NATIONAL HISPANIC HERITAGE MONTH
SEPTEMBER 15–OCTOBER 15

what is Hispanic Heritage Month

Hispanic Heritage Month is celebrated from September 15 to October 15 in the U.S., honoring the histories, cultures, and contributions of Hispanic and Latino Americans.

The Start of the Celebration

Marcos woke up with excitement bubbling inside him. Today marked the beginning of Hispanic Heritage Month, a time to celebrate the rich culture and traditions of his family and neighbors. His mom had decorated the house with colorful papel picado banners, and the delicious smell of freshly baked empanadas filled the air.

Marcos hurriedly dressed in his favorite guayabera shirt and joined his family in the kitchen. His dad was busy making tamales, while his younger sister, Sofia, was helping to set up the table with vibrant plates and cups. They were preparing for a big neighborhood party later that day.

As the sun rose higher in the sky, neighbors started arriving at Marcos's house, each bringing their own special dishes and decorations. There were piñatas, maracas, and flowers everywhere. Marcos felt a sense of pride and joy seeing everyone come together to celebrate their heritage

A Day of Music and Dance

The party kicked off with music from a live mariachi band. Marcos and his friends couldn't resist the lively rhythms and soon found themselves dancing along. The sound of guitars, trumpets, and violins filled the air, making everyone tap their feet and sway to the beat.

Marcos's abuela, who was known for her storytelling, gathered the children around her. She shared tales of her own childhood and the traditions she grew up with in Mexico. The kids listened in awe, learning about the significance of the Day of the Dead, the vibrant parades, and the importance of family.

As the sun set, it was time for the traditional dance performance. Marcos and his friends had been practicing for weeks, and they were eager to show off their skills. Dressed in traditional costumes, they performed folklorico dances, twirling and stomping in perfect harmony, to the delight of the audience.

Sharing Traditions

The next morning, Marcos and his family visited their local community center, which was hosting a Hispanic Heritage Month exhibition. There were displays of traditional clothing, crafts, and artifacts from various Hispanic cultures. Marcos loved seeing the vibrant textiles and intricate pottery.

Marcos participated in a workshop where he learned to make his own papel picado banners. With a piece of tissue paper and a pair of scissors, he carefully cut out beautiful patterns. He felt a deep connection to his heritage, knowing that he was continuing a tradition that had been passed down through generations.

In the afternoon, there was a cooking demonstration where local chefs shared their recipes for traditional dishes. Marcos watched as they prepared ceviche, arepas, and flan. He even got to taste some of the delicious food, savoring the rich flavors and spices that reminded him of his family's kitchen.

A Community United

As the month-long celebration continued, Marcos noticed how the festivities brought the community closer together. People from different backgrounds joined in, learning about and appreciating Hispanic culture. The neighborhood felt more connected and vibrant than ever before.

One of the highlights of the month was the grand parade. Floats decorated with flowers, dancers in traditional costumes, and musicians filled the streets with color and sound. Marcos proudly marched alongside his friends, waving flags and smiling at the cheering crowd.

On the final night of the celebration, the community gathered for a grand fiesta. There were fireworks, more delicious food, and lots of dancing. As Marcos looked around at his family, friends, and neighbors, he felt a deep sense of gratitude and pride. Hispanic Heritage Month had been a wonderful journey of discovery, celebration, and unity.

What did Marcos wake up excited about?

A) His birthday
B) Hispanic Heritage Month
C) A school trip

What delicious smell filled the air at Marcos's house?

A) Pancakes
B) Pizza
C) Empanadas

What did Marcos wear for the celebration?

A) A superhero costume
B) His favorite guayabera shirt
C) A sports jersey

What type of music kicked off the party?

A) Rock music
B) Jazz music
C) Mariachi music

Who shared stories of her childhood with the children?

A) Marcos's mom
B) Marcos's abuela
C) Marcos's teacher

What did Marcos and his friends perform in the evening?

A) A magic show
B) Folklorico dances
C) A play

What did Marcos learn to make at the community center workshop?

A) Pottery
B) Papel picado banners
C) Sculptures

What was one of the highlights of the month-long celebration?

A) A sports tournament
B) A grand parade
C) A movie night

Made in the USA
Columbia, SC
10 January 2025